A **Fruitful People**

DISCIPLING PENTECOSTALS
200 SERIES Volume 3

A **Fruitful** **People**

A Pentecostal Study on Bearing the Fruit of the Spirit

Wilmer Estrada-Carraquillo

ISBN: 978-1-940682-75-4

TABLE OF CONTENTS

ACKNOWLEDGMENTS

I want to begin by expressing my gratitude to our God and Savior. Beyond the research and writing hours along with all the nuances that make possible a project like this, all begins and ends with God's mercy and grace. This book is a testimony of God's continuous work in me.

Also, I would like to say thank you to Reverend Pamela R. Brewer and Dr. O. Wayne Brewer. Thanks for the invitation to join in an enriching project such as this. I have always told myself that I wanted to bless the church with the fruit of writing and scholarship that God has placed within me. And, to do so with men and women like the ones who are contributers of this series which makes it even better.

Moreover, I am grateful for my pastors and local church. As I was writing this book, they became a sounding board by way of pew conversations, preaching, and teaching. Their feedback and encouragement pushed me through difficult moments during the writing phase.

Furthermore, I want to recognize PTS, the Pentecostal Theological Seminary, the Center for Latino Studies, and the Centre for Pentecostal Theology. These educational communities offered valuable space, time, and resources that helped me to complete this project.

Finally, I want to say thank you to God for His gift of love to me, Laura and our daughters—Kalani Sofia, Mia Kamila and Valeria Kamil. Their understanding and generosity were not only a gift for me, but also for everyone who will read this book.

—Wilmer Estrada Carrasquillo

FOREWORD

Why Have a Series on Discipling Pentecostals?

Why indeed? Why disciple "Pentecostals"... specifically? Quite simply because Pentecostal (and charismatic) Christianity is such an explosive and powerfully growing segment of Christ's Church in the world today! John Allen, in the *National Catholic Reporter* calls the growth of the Pentecostal church a "Pentecostal Explosion."[1] Ralph Martin has said, "My research has led me to make a bold statement: In all of human history, no other non-political, non-militaristic, voluntary human movement has grown as rapidly as the Pentecostal-Charismatic Movement in the last 25 years.[2] In a Per Forum on Religion and Public Life, a study of countries in Asia, North America, Africa, South America, and Central America led to Luis Lugo, director of the Pew Study, to say, "I don't think it is too far-fetched to seriously consider whether Christianity is well on its way to being Pentecostalized."[3] In fact, Wesley Granberg-Michaelson now says that "Globally, one of four Christians in the world now identify as Pentecostal-Charismatic, with Pentecostalism growing at roughly four times the rate of the world's population."[4]

Both Pentecostal disciples and Pentecostal disciple-makers take Jesus' words in Matthew 16:18 literally when He said ". . . I will build my church; and the gates of hell shall not prevail against it." If asked why the Pentecostal church is making so many disciples around the world, a Pentecostal believer might well respond: "It is because of the power of the Holy Spirit and the fulfillment of the prophet Joel's prophecy that in the latter days, the Lord will "pour out" His Spirit "upon all flesh." His Spirit is indeed essential to the Great Commission task of disciple-making.

Discipling Pentecostals is a "200-level" follow-up series to the original Living What We Believe series, which is a six-volume entry-level series loosely based on the "Fivefold Gospel" paradigm of Jesus as Savior, Sanctifier, Spirit-Baptizer, Healer, and Coming King." Discipling Pentecostals is the logical extension of this doctrinal foundation. Making disciples is all about developing true followers of Jesus Christ while understanding that the person and work of the Holy Spirit is intimately and undeniably involved in this lifelong process. It is the Holy Spirit who enables disciples to become more like Jesus. Thus, the six volumes of Discipling Pentecostals literally highlight six essential Pentecostal attributes which characterize a true disciple of Jesus Christ.

These volumes are:

- Volume One—*A Praying People: A Pentecostal Study of the Vital Prayer Life* (highlighting various types and dynamics of scriptural praying) by Lee Roy Martin.

- Volume Two—*An Overcoming People: A Pentecostal Study for Victorious Spiritual Warfare* (highlighting scriptural teaching/dynamics of spiritual warfare) by O. Wayne Brewer.

- Volume Three—*A Fruitful People: A Pentecostal Study on Bearing the Fruit of the Spirit* (highlighting the nine-fold fruit of the spiritual life) by Wilmer Estrada-Carrasquillo.

- Volume Four—*A Gifted People: A Pentecostal Study for the Use of the Gifts of the Spirit* (highlighting the multiplicity and usage of spiritual gifts primarily in Paul's Epistles) by French L. Arrington.

- Volume Five—*A Blessed People: A Pentecostal Study for Living Out the Beatitudes* (highlighting Jesus' teaching on the Beatitudes) by Lee Roy Martin.

- Volume Six—*A Miraculous People: A Pentecostal Study on Expecting Miracles* (highlighting Old Testament and New Testament teachings and narratives dealing with signs, wonders, miracles, and divine healing) by Miriam E. Figueroa.

These six attributes are some (but certainly not all) of the essential, characteristics of Pentecostal disciple-making:

1. The priority of praying.
2. The necessity of victorious spiritual warfare.
3. Bearing the fruit of the Spirit.
4. Being open to the Spirit's operation of spiritual gifts.
5. Living as a blessed, Kingdom people.
6. Expecting the miracles which were, and continue to be, a genuine part of Christ's ministry in and through His Church.

How Does This Series on Discipling Pentecostals Work?

This six-volume series of small group/class studies is written and specifically developed for the purpose of making Pentecostal disciples of Jesus Christ. For those seeking to *know* more about living the Christlike life, there is plenty here to be learned and discussed. However, this series (all six-volumes) has much more to offer than biblical knowledge and doctrine alone. This series has been especially created to foster relational discipleship within a community of believers for the purpose of transformational life change!

Discipling Pentecostals is a complete 24-week disciple-ship study (though participants or groups are free to use any one volume alone, or in any order they prefer). This series both understands and is built upon the truth that only disciples make other disciples! Coming together as the body of Christ within the context of a small group is an essential and fruitful means by which Jesus' Great Commission (Matthew 28:18-20) can be fulfilled. Likewise, coming together as the body of Christ within the context of a small group is also a natural and organic means by which Jesus' Great Commandment (Matthew 22:36-40) can find a more productive fulfillment.

Over the course of the six volumes of this series, the reader/participant will be provided with biblical/doctrinal teaching based on a number of key scriptural passages, as well as the opportunity to reflect upon and discuss the practical ramifications of living out the Spirit-filled Christlike life . . . all within the relational context of small group discipleship.

The format of the Discipling Pentecostals series is simple, relational, and structured specifically to make true disciples, as well as assisting disciple-makers to fulfill their mission. Each of the six volumes is a four-week study with each week divided into five days. Each participant reads, reflects, and reacts to each of these days at home in his or her personal time. Each day will feature several components which enable the growth process of the disciple at a personal level:

1. "Search the Scripture" (selected Scripture readings).
2. "Answer the Following Questions" (reflective questions which are directly relevant to the Scripture selection).
3. "Yield to the Spirit" (divided into three subsections):
   - *Know:* Relating to one's intellect—your "head." This is orthodoxy (right doctrine/truth).
   - *Be:* Relating to one's passion—your "heart." This is orthopathy (right passions/affections).
   - *Do:* Relating to one's behavior—your "hands." This is orthopraxy (right living/behavior).
4. "Offer a Prayer" (the conclusion of each day).

After the five daily personal interactions, the participant will join with the other members (who have likewise personally worked through the sessions) for the weekly small group session. Led by the leader/facilitator, the weekly small group meetings provide members with the time to open up, give responses, and yield to the corporate and personal leading of the Holy Spirit. The leader/facilitator does not decide the response from members, but rather, asks questions and helps guide group members to the practical, behavioral outworking of what we believe as Pentecostal members of the body of Christ. Each group session is about sharing, relating, learning, and being aware of the presence of the Holy Spirit. There will be a key scripture for discussion in each group session. As you work through the studies, you will note information about the "Opening," Prayer," "Testimony," Discussion Questions," and the section we refer to as "Yielding to the Spirit." Group leaders will find much more very helpful information concerning both starting and leading a small group from series Assistant Editor J. Ben Wiles in the following sections of this volume. If you are a group leader/facilitator, always make sure to publicly welcome the presence of the Holy Spirit to guide, teach, convict, encourage, and unify all those who are present for the weekly group session. Remember that the ultimate benefits of the Discipling Pentecostals Discipleship Series are not only the transmission of biblical/doctrinal teaching, but also the Spirit-led, life-transformation of men and women into healthy disciples of Jesus Christ!

As general editor and publishers of this disciple-making series, we wish to express our thanks and sincere appreciation to Assistant Editor J. Ben Wiles, whose *People of the Spirit* served as the primary template for Discipling Pentecostals. We also wish to thank Lenae Simmons for her diligent labor in the copy editing, layout, and design of this work. Finally, we wish to convey our respect and gratitude to the scholars who authored the individual volumes:

- Volume One—Lee Roy Martin
- Volume Two—O. Wayne Brewer
- Volume Three—Wilmer Estrada-Carrasquillo
- Volume Four—French L. Arrington
- Volume Five—Lee Roy Martin
- Volume Six—Miriam E. Figueroa

These authors and their insightful work and commitment of making disciples for Jesus Christ cannot be overstated. You will appreciate their scholarship and enjoy their insights into God's Word!

Whether Pentecostal, Evangelical, or any believer who wishes to take up the cross and follow Jesus, we highly recommend all six volumes of the Discipling Pentecostals series. If you are a disciple-maker, this series is for you. While it can certainly be used for individual study, we highly recommend the small group experience.

O. Wayne Brewer, D.Min., Int. Men's Discipleship Director
Pamela R. Brewer, M.A., Int. Women's Discipleship Director

Adult Discipleship, Church of God International Offices

General Editors: O. Wayne and Pamela R. Brewer
Assistant Editor: J. Ben Wiles
Chief Copy Editor: Layout and Design: Lenae Simmons

FOREWORD ENDNOTES

[1] John Allen, *National Catholic Reporter* (January 28, 2008) *ncronline.org/news/if-demography-destiny-pentecostal-are-ecumenical-future,* accessed, July 25, 2015.

[2] Ralph Martin, *The Catholic Church at the End of the Age: What the Spirit Is Saying,* (San Francisco: Ignatius, 1994) 87.

[3] Luis Lugo, *Spirit and Power: A 10-Country Survey of Pentecostals, pewforum.org/files/2006/pentecostals-08.pdf.* accessed July 20, 2015.

[4] Wesley Granberg-Michaelson, "Future Faith: Ten Challenges Reshaping Christianity in the 21st Century," (*Church of God Evangel* (March 2019, Cleveland, Tennessee: Pathway Press) 9.

PREFACE

How to Start a Small Group

The following steps are important in the process of starting a group in your local church:

1. Pray and seek the leadership of the Holy Spirit to make sure He is calling you to lead a small group.

2. Secure permission from the pastor of your local church to lead the group.

3. Find an appropriate location that is conducive to the group encounters—either in the church facility or in a host home. Public areas such as coffee shops are not appropriate, as they would potentially hinder the group's ability to fully engage the leading of the Spirit during times of prayer.

4. Set a time and place for the first meeting.

5. Develop the group through invitation. Your goal is clear: to lead every member of the group to grow in Jesus Christ, and to discover and fulfill God's personal call on his or her life in the power of the Holy Spirit. This is a transformation group where every member will grow and be fully involved in the discipleship process personally and by leading others in the discipleship process. Select four or, at most, five people to be in your group. Include at least one mature believer and at least one new believer. (Note: a group with four to five people is best

for a study such as this one. However, if you need to have a larger group, you should not have more than 10 to 12 people).

6. Decide how you are going to handle childcare.

7. Determine the cost for the group. Group members should purchase their own copy of the student guides for each unit, unless the church has opted to make other arrangements.

8. Order materials in plenty of time to have them for the first group encounter.

9. Read through the leader's guide and acclimate yourself to the small group process.

Keys to Successfully Leading a Small Group

1. Get to know the group members.

2. Encourage participation by everyone. Remember that discipleship and lecturing are not the same thing. You are a facilitator, and your job is to facilitate participation that leads to transformation for everyone!

   • Communicate your expectation that everyone participates.

   • Ask questions.

   • Make it fulfilling so they want to return.

   • Reduce and eliminate embarrassing and threatening situations.

   • Protect and honor confidentiality within the group.

3. Affirming vs. Endorsing

   • It is important that, as the leader, you affirm all the responses. You say, "Thank you, Ben," or "That's very interesting, Elizabeth." No matter what the participants say, don't criticize their remarks. What they just said may be antagonistic to you or it may simply sound ridiculous, but don't directly criticize it. Instead, say some thing like, "Well, that's interesting. What do the rest of you think?" Once you, as the leader, directly disapprove of someone's comments, then some people will never speak up again. They're going to fear disapproval; once exploration stops for them, the journey does too. On the other side of the coin, while it's important to affirm all responses, avoid the temptation to endorse them. Don't say things like, "Now that's a great comment," or "I couldn't agree with you more." Such endorsements tip your hand and leave others feeling like their comments are not acceptable. Also, resist the urge to be too instructional, trying to answer everyone's questions and solve everyone's problems. Once a know-it-all person speaks up, conversation tends to shut down. You can give your own opinion, but do it in a personal and humble way. Maybe you could say, "My experience has been . . ." or "This is how I see it . . ."

4. Remember the four C's of the facilitator's role:

* **Content**—Keep the group grounded in Scripture.

* **Care**—Be sensitive to the feelings, needs, and life situations of the group members.

* **Commitment**—Demonstrate your commitment to completing the Living What We Believe process completely and thoroughly. Model your commitment by your careful preparation as the facilitator for each of the group encounters.

* **Consistency**—Follow up consistently with established schedules and routines for the group. Your consistent approach to the process will inspire the same in the participants. Also, a consistently positive attitude will go a long way to establishing a healthy environment for the group to flourish.

5. Manage difficult and challenging personalities in your group so they don't hijack the encounters.

- The Talking Hijacker answers every question before anyone else can respond. In her book, *Help! My Small Group Has Been Hijacked!, Four Common Hijackers and ways to Respond*, Margaret Feinberg discusses helpful responses to potential small group "Hijackings."

    o Your first course of action is to pull them aside in a one-on-one meeting. Thank them for their participation, but be honest with them about the need for others to participate. Consider some practical ways you could offer to help them do that (respond only to every second or third question, keep responses short, and so forth).

    o Your second course of action (if the first course of action doesn't work) is to change the discussion time to a more structured format. For example, you call on people for answers.

- The Emotional Hijacker shows up every week with an emotional crisis.

    o The first course of action is to spend some one-on-one time with this person and allow him or her to emotionally unpack with you. If necessary, recommend a good counselor or a conversation with the pastor. This may alleviate the problem in the group encounter.

    o If the first course of action doesn't resolve the issue, you may need to remind the group of the task at hand, which is to work through the material, and that extra questions can be raised at the end of the session.

- ○ **Note**: there may be a person in your group who is just going through a difficult time and is not truly an emotional hijacker. Be open to the leading of the Holy Spirit to allow a short time of personal ministry to this person if you feel it is appropriate; then return to the material at hand for that group encounter.

6. The Leader Hijacker is a backseat driver who is constantly making suggestions about how you should lead the group.

   - ◆ The first course of action is to have a one-on-one conversation with the individual. Sift through his or her comments to see if you can glean anything helpful. Sometimes, there will be good suggestions that can benefit the group. If so, mention these helpful suggestions in your conversation, which will keep the atmosphere positive. Politely ask the leader hijacker to stop doing so at the group encounters by pointing out that he/she can lead to disunity in the group.

   - ◆ If the hijacker does it in another meeting, simply say, "We can talk about suggestions outside of the group encounter," then continue with the material at hand.

7. The Late Hijacker constantly walks into the group encounter late, disrupting the group and causing a loss of momentum and focus.

   - ◆ Discuss the situation directly with the individual and encourage him or her to make every effort to arrive on time. If that is not possible, encourage him or her to arrive quietly and discreetly so as to not disturb the group. They should also consider waiting outside if it seems to be a particularly sensitive moment.

- If the individual continues to disrupt the group, consider privately encouraging them to find another group to join that would work better with his or her schedule.

8. Remember, you are accountable for your stewardship of the group!

- Care for them enough that you refuse to accept poor decisions or justification for inconsistent participation.

- Don't be judgmental. Address behaviors only— don't try to guess the motivation behind them.

- Pray regularly over the group.

- See yourself as a mentor/role model.

- Encourage authentic relationships and conversations in the group by modeling them. Be yourself and be real, but also be holy and be humble!

- Trust God. Whatever is accomplished is by Him and through Him and for His glory. It is His will for you and your group to succeed and He is ready to give you the grace to do so!

Group Covenant

Instead, speaking the truth in love, we will grow to become in every respect the mature body of him who is the head, that is, Christ. From him the whole body, joined and held together by every supporting ligament, grows and builds itself up in love, as each part does its work (Ephesians 4:15-16 NIV).

It is hoped that each individual undertaking the small group process will experience transformation and growth in Christlikeness over the course of the experience. But individual growth alone is not enough. It must take place in the context of relationship with others of the same faith, each one building the others up so that all become mature followers of Jesus Christ and, as a result, fully functioning participants in God's plan to save creation. With that in mind, before continuing with the study, each member of the group should agree to the following covenant with one another. Please read and reflect upon the following statements and indicate your commitment to the group by signing your name at the bottom. Then each member of the small group should sign one another's group covenant so that everyone's copy has every signature of the group. Keep this group covenant in your book for future reference as needed.

GROUP COVENANT

PRIORITY: The group meeting will be a priority in my schedule. If I am running late or unable to attend, I will contact my group leader.

PREPAREDNESS: I realize that what I put into the lesson is what I will get out of it. Therefore, I will prepare for the lesson each week and come prepared to share.

RESPECT: Everyone has a right to his or her opinion and all questions are encouraged and respected. I will listen attentively to others without interrupting them.

CONFIDENTIALITY: Anything of a personal nature that is said in the meeting should not be repeated outside the meeting. This group is intended to be a safe place for open discussion and sharing.

HONESTY: I will strive to be real, honest, and transparent with the other group members.

SUPPORT: The mission and values of the group have my support, and I will refrain from gossip or criticism.

SIGNATURES   DATE

INTRODUCTION
The Farmer, the Seed, and the Soil

I was born and raised in Puerto Rico. For a time, Puerto Rican economy, like many of its neighboring countries in the Caribbean, was sustained in large part by the agricultural industry. My grandparent's generation and those before them, raised their families with the fruit of their labor. That labor was not easy! It was hard labor, but it produced good fruit. This did not happen under a climate-controlled room—like the one from where I am writing this book. Each day, they walked into the fields and worked the soil with their beat-up hands in order to produce fruit.

From time to time, I recall some of the stories that my grandfather Papito shared with me. This book prompted one of those stories—his life was lived as a man of the land (a farmer). We usually visited our grandparents every Sunday afternoon. There were times when we arrived, Papito was walking out of his field all dirty and sweaty; nevertheless, his face was joyful from spending time in his little piece of land. I learned through his experience as a farmer, that working the land brings with it a mixture of exhaustion and gratification. "It takes so much work to plant a field like that," says Papito as he points to the field where he toils across the street from his home. Then he continued, "but when I come back, not only with my tools, but also with a cluster of plantains, that brings me so much joy."

As I remember Papito's words, I cannot stop thinking that though there are times when his hands would feel the pain and stress of beating, seeding, fertilizing, and irrigating the soil, those same hands, in a span of time, would also carry the joy and fruit of his labor. It seems that the possibility of holding in his hand the fruit of his labor, was the source of his strength during the long days of work under the drenching Caribbean rains, hot sunny days, itchy mosquito bites, and weakening humidity. What is more interesting is, whatever joy he experienced as he carried the fruit; he was ready to start it all over again. I guess he did not want a land that just bore fruit. He wanted a fruit-giving land, i.e., a land that would be fruitful. That would only be possible if he continuously worked the land.

This book will take us through a similar journey. Using the words of the apostle Paul to the church in Galatia, *A Fruitful People* seeks to take us into a journey of bearing good fruit. "So I [Paul] say, walk by the Spirit" (Galatians 5:16 NIV). And in doing so, we will walk contrary to the desires of the flesh and will be "led by the Spirit" (Galatians 5:18). If we opt to keep walking in the Spirit, we will not act according to the flesh (Galatians 5:19), but we will be on a fruit-giving journey. That is the journey to which the apostle is inviting both the Galatians and us. It is a journey that is characterized by the fruit of the Spirit. In his words,

> But the fruit of the Spirit is love, joy, peace, patience, kindness, goodness, faithfulness, gentleness and self-control. Against such things there is no law. Those who belong to Christ Jesus have crucified the flesh with its pas-sions and desires. Since we live by the Spirit, let us keep in step with the Spirit. Let us not become conceited, provoking and envying each other (Galatians 5:22-26).

The "fruit of the Spirit" is an allegorical expression that the Scriptures use to describe the Christlike virtues or graces that are manifested in the lives of Christians. As the name implies this fruit comes from, and is cultivated by the Holy Spirit who indwells all believers. For this fruit to mature (just like fruit in nature), time and cultivation are needed. Just as the sun, water, and minerals from the earth eventually produce delicious, fragrant, healthy, and colorful fruit for people to enjoy, so also does the Son, the "living water," and the applied life-giving Words of God produce the fruit of the Spirit in the lives of Christians. The Holy Spirit who lives in us will cultivate and produce this Christ-glorifying fruit when we live and walk in the Spirit. Life is sweeter, others' lives are touched, and Jesus Christ is glorified when we bear the fruit of the Spirit!

In John 15:1-16, Jesus taught at some length about the responsibilities of believers to bear fruit. He taught that those who abide in Him and who in turn allow Him to abide in them will bear fruit—much fruit. Read John 15 closely. In verses 12 and 13 Jesus emphasizes love. You will see that in studying the fruit of the Spirit, it is crucial to remember that the fruit of the Spirit is really one fruit whose core in an unselfish, God-given love. All the nine different aspects or graces of the fruit of the Spirit are a single, love-based unity. With this in mind, we see how the love of Christ, as evidenced by the fruit of the Spirit, is the beautiful evidence of a mature, growing, Christ-centered, Spirit-led disciple. After all, Jesus said in Luke 6:44 that "each tree is recognized by its own fruit."

Let us join together in this Spirit-driven journey. As we do, I pray for two simple things: First, that this book becomes like the seed that was scattered by the farmer. Second, that our hearts will be the good soil, and as we journey through this discipling experience, the yield becomes "a hundred times more than was sown" (Luke 8:8). Let us labor together in the Spirit!

WEEK ONE

༄

The Farmer, the Seed, and the Soil

WEEK ONE
The Farmer, the Seed, and the Soil

Day 1
Let Us Gather Closely

Touching Base

Welcome to Day 1 of our first week! Before we move into an in-depth study of the Galatians 5 passage, I believe that it will be in order to prepare our hearts for the seed that will be sown in them as we come together as a community of faith and study God's inspired Word. Each day we will not only search the Scriptures with selected readings and make use of reflective questions, but we will also engage in yielding to the Spirit. By this, we are saying that we will discuss each day's lesson by addressing how it affects our intellect (Know), our passions (Be), and behavior (Do).

As you might have read in the preface, this book is part of a series called Discipling Pentecostals. From my point of view, the series title points are two important elements that we need to keep in mind as we take on this journey. On the one hand, the usage of the term discipling denotes that we are in a continuous path of learning, the *ing* ending affirms this. Hence, to accept the call to be a disciple is to accept a journey that has no finish line in terms of learning. On the other hand, the kind of learning that we will have is circumscribed by a Pentecostal approach and experience. Though there are few methods that can be used for this approach, I will settle on one that will be helpful for the task at hand—an integration of Word, Spirit, and community. Therefore, as we embark on this journey let us continually be immersed in a learning experience which is *founded* in the Word, *guided* by the Spirit and *lived out* in community.

Searching the Scripture

> While a large crowd was gathering and people were coming to Jesus from town after town, he told this parable: "A farmer went out to sow his seed. As he was scattering the seed, some fell along the path; it was trampled on, and the birds ate it up. Some fell on rocky ground, and when it came up, the plants withered because they had no moisture. Other seed fell among thorns, which grew up with it and choked the plants. Still other seed fell on good soil. It came up and yielded a crop, a hundred times more than was sown." When he said this, he called out, "Whoever has ears to hear, let them hear" (Luke 8:4-8).

Answer the Following Questions:

Now that you have meditated on some of these points or those that the Spirit placed in your heart, take time to answer the following questions. Approach these as guiding questions that will help you move deeper into a discerning process.

1. Do you have a farmer story? How does it speak to you in light of this text?

2. Why do you think many people were coming to Jesus?

3. How does your understanding of this parable change when you see the farmer as a representation of Jesus and the seed as a representation of the Word?

Yielding to the Spirit

> While a large crowd was gathering and people were coming to Jesus from town after town, he told this parable: "A farmer went out to sow his seed . . ."

—Know—

Jesus' words were not like the words of any other teacher! His words, according to Luke 8:1, were words that proclaimed "the good news of the kingdom of God." According to Luke's narrative, in His visit to the synagogue (Luke 4), Jesus affirms that His mission is to fulfill God's kingdom. He was clear about His mission, and He knew the importance of it. It would be a Kingdom embodied and manifested in Jesus' life and ministry (Luke 4:21).

Furthermore, Jesus' teaching methods stood contrary to those used by other teachers! He not only spoke to a select group of male disciples that followed Him (as it was the practice of that time), but also Jesus' proclamation was for all who wanted to hear. Indeed, Jesus had an inner circle who were later called the apostles, yet, He did not limit His teaching to them. And Luke, who seems to expand the number of those who were following Jesus, begins Chapter 8 by recognizing, the Twelve, some women, a large crowd, and people who were "coming to Jesus from town after town" (Luke 8:4). How important it is to know that God's words are for all who have ears to hear.

—Be—

Jesus begins the parable stating the following, "A farmer went out to sow his seed" (Luke 8:5). This is a quick phrase that we can overlook; however, there are a couple of important things we need to understand, especially if we compare (in any way) the farmer to a representation of Jesus himself. The farmer, as in the story I shared about Papito, cannot sow the seed unless he goes out. There is, in essence the innate responsibility to go out to the field if, in any way, the seed is to find a place where it can grow and give fruit. If Papito would have stood on the other side of the street and thrown the seed, it would have fallen short of the field, and the seed would have fallen in its entirety on the street. Instead, he went out to the field, and then he sowed the seed. In a way, Jesus is coming to us in the form of this book.

—Do—

A second point that comes out of the opening phrase of the parable is that the seed is of the farmer, "to sow his seed." The importance of this point does not lie in the idea of ownership, but it lies in the source of the seed. Remember, the imagery of the farmer, the seed, and the soil are used as a figure of speech to point to a greater message. Hence, if the farmer stands in the parable as Jesus, he is not only the one who went out, but also, he is sowing his seed, which in this case, stands for the Word of God. Such an understanding is important because the seed in itself, without a shadow of a doubt, bears fruit within it. It is a living word (seed). Similarly, to what I said above, he is not only coming to us, but also planting his seed as we gather as a learning community.

Take time to reflect on what has been said. Do so with a discerning disposition and open heart. If needed, use the bullet points below. Feel free to add other important points that I might have overlooked. Ask the Holy Spirit to speak into you and your peers' lives. Discipling denotes that we are in a continuous path of learning.

- A Pentecostal learning experience is founded in the Word, guided by the Spirit, and lived out in community.

- Jesus' words proclaimed the good news of the kingdom of God.

- Jesus' proclamation was for all who wanted to hear.

- The Spirit of the Lord anointed Jesus to speak and do the mission of God in this world.

- Jesus utilized parables to motivate His hearers to make wise choices in life.

- The farmer cannot sow the seed unless he goes out.

- The farmer is sowing his seed, which, in this case, stands for the Word of God.

Offer a Prayer

Dear Father, we thank You that You sent out Your Son in the power of the Holy Spirit to sow the seed of the Word in us. We want to draw close to You and be part of the people who gather around You so we can receive the seed being sown. Help us, oh God, we want to have ears that hear the Word. Amen!

Day 2
Watch Out for the Birds

Touching Base

Welcome to Day 2! In the previous chapter, we discussed the farmer having a seed of his own that he wanted to sow. Now in order to grow, the seed must be sown in a soil that will have the necessary nutrients that will nurture the seed.

Today marks one of four days that we will study the different places where the farmer's seed fell. What we will learn in the following days is, the farmer's seed is good seed; yet, the possibility of growing and bearing fruit is contingent on the ground where the seed will fall.

The psalmist helps us to understand this when he states in Psalm 1 that a blessed person is the one who is, "planted by streams of water, which yields its fruit in season and whose leaf does not wither—whatever they do prospers" (Psalm 1:3). This particular seed was planted in a good place. It received the necessary nutrients from the soil, making it a tree that not only yielded fruit but also did not wither. But, watch out, if the seed is scattered in a place which is not prepared to nurture it, it can be stepped on and eaten by the birds.

Searching the Scripture

While a large crowd was gathering and people were coming to Jesus from town after town, he told this parable: "A farmer went out to sow his seed. As he was scattering the seed, some fell along the path; it was trampled on, and the birds ate it up. Some fell on rocky ground, and when it came up, the plants withered because they had no moisture. Other seed fell among thorns, which grew up with it and choked the plants. Still other seed fell on good soil. It came up and yielded a crop, a hundred times more than was sown." When he said this, he called out, "Whoever has ears to hear, let them hear" (Luke 8:4-8.)

Answer the Following Questions:

Meditate on the introduction and scripture that you have read, but specifically in the section that was highlighted. As you do, ponder the following questions:

1. What other things do we find in a path that can hinder the growth of seed?

2. How can the "birds" put the scattered seed in danger?

3. What is the Spirit saying to you today?

Yielding to the Spirit

> As he was scattering the seed, some fell along the
> path; it was trampled on, and the birds ate it up
> (Luke 8:5).

—*Know*—

One of the questions that surfaced as I was studying this text was: Why does the farmer scatter the seed on the ground which will be walked over? Interestingly, the majority of biblical scholars who comment on this text mention that the "The Palestinian sower sowed first and ploughed (plowed) afterwards."[1] That means that some of the seed would not bear fruit as it would be walked over or would be damaged as the farmer came later and plowed the ground. Regardless, the seed was not retained; it was scattered all over.

—*Be*—

There is no time and space to discuss Palestinian agricultural techniques, but one thing is certain, the farmer sowed plentifully and without any hesitation. He scattered as much seed as possible, which gave him the opportunity for a plentiful yield. Know this: God is a plentiful sower. We should be thankful for that, because we are part of that harvest. The Father sent Jesus for all people without hesitation, knowing that His Son would make a way for all to

WEEK ONE—THE FARMER, THE SEED, AND THE SOIL

come to the Father. Similarly, that is how we ought to be able to give ourselves to all in order to enhance the opportunity of bearing fruit.

—Do—

Contemporary forms of agriculture show that the soil is prepared before the seed is scattered. Maybe it is a good time to see the condition of our mind, heart, and soul. The farmer is scattering seed upon us! The seed is a fruitful seed! Come, Holy Spirit, plow us for the seed that is being sowed.

Offer a Prayer

Holy Spirit, make us aware of the things that can trample God's Word in us. Let's take care of the seed of the Word and watch out for the birds that want to take away what You have given us. Amen!

Day 3
Do Not Lose Your Moisture

Touching Base

Welcome to Day 3! In the previous chapter, we were warned about the birds that are seeking to take the seed that has been scattered. One way of doing this is by preparing ourselves for the sowing season. Keeping our ground watered, is a central part of this process. When we don't, there is not much hope for the seed to grow.

Searching the Scripture

While a large crowd was gathering and people were coming to Jesus from town after town, he told this parable: "A farmer went out to sow his seed. As he was scattering the seed, some fell along the path; it was trampled on, and the birds ate it up. Some fell on rocky ground, and when it came up, the plants withered because they had no moisture. Other seed fell among thorns, which grew up with it and choked the plants. Still other seed fell on good soil. It came up and yielded a crop, a hundred times more than was sown." When he said this, he called out, "Whoever has ears to hear, let them hear" (Luke 8:4-8).

Answer the Following Questions:

Meditate on the introduction and Scripture passage that you have read, but specifically in the section that was highlighted. As you do, ponder the following questions:

1. What things do you see growing in your life that are in need of care?

2. Can you name what "rock-like" issues can cause your heart to become dry?

3. How would you water your life spiritually in time of dryness?

Yielding to the Spirit

> Some fell on rocky ground, and when it came up,
> the plants withered because they had no moisture
> (Luke 8: 6).

—*Know*—

As I read this section of the parable, I was amazed at the resiliency of the seed that was being sowed. The parable tells us that this seed is capable of growing even in rocky ground. In contrast to the previous section, the seed never got opportunity to grow past the surface level. But occasionally, regardless of the ground, once the seed had opportunity to be "buried," its possibilities of growing were a reality.

According to the text, the rocky ground had in it the possibilities of giving life to the seed. And it did. Yet, this was not enough; the rocky ground by itself was not able to sustain the plant. The rocky ground can become so dry that it can quickly disturb the growth of that to which it had given life. That is why the moisture is needed. We can keep our ground watered only as we come closer to Jesus.

—*Be*—

I can't stop thinking of Jesus' encounter with the Samaritan woman at the well. In their conversation, she demonstrated some understanding of what it meant to worship God. However, there was something missing. Paraphrasing the words of Jesus: She was worshiping what she didn't know. The seed planted in her, though, demonstrated some signs of growth and life; but in reality, it was withering.

Her life was at a difficult crossroads; consequently, Jesus offered to water her. The water she was about to get from the well wouldn't last long; it wouldn't quench her thirst. In response, Jesus offered her the opportunity to drink from the source of everlasting water—one that would moisturize her rocky and dry life. If she drank from the Jesus' water, it would never run dry. As Jesus himself said, you "will never thirst" (John 4:14).

—Do—

The Samaritan woman had two choices. First, she could reject the opportunity of drinking the water that would quench her thirst forever and keep coming to Jacob's well. Second, she could drop the jar, make that trip to Jesus' "well" and accept His invitation. As we all know, she did the latter. Her decision to do so, made it possible for the seed to grow in her and bear fruit, to the point that she went back to her community, shared the good news to all, and they believed.

Offer a Prayer

Jesus, let the living water that runs from You inundate our lives every day. Help us to leave our jars behind and welcome the stream of Your words running though our dry and rocky hearts so Your seed may bear fruit as it did with the Samaritan woman. Amen!

Day 4
Be Aware of the Thorns

Touching Base

Welcome to Day 4! To this point we have talked about the importance of caring for the seed, protecting them from the birds, and about not losing our moisture. Today, we will turn to another precautionary segment of the parable, i.e., be aware of the thorns. While the birds may eat the seed and the lack of moisture may dry up the sprouted seed, the thorns are known for choking them. May the Spirit speak to us this week.

Searching the Scripture

While a large crowd was gathering and people were coming to Jesus from town after town, he told this parable: "A farmer went out to sow his seed. As he was scattering the seed, some fell along the path; it was trampled on, and the birds ate it up. Some fell on rocky ground, and when it came up, the plants withered because they had no moisture. Other seed fell among thorns, which grew up with it and choked the plants. Still other seed fell on good soil. It came up and yielded a crop, a hundred times more than was sown." When he said this, he called out, "Whoever has ears to hear, let them hear" (Luke 8:4-8).

Answer the Following Questions:

After reading this week's introductory words and biblical text, meditate on the following questions and answer them:

1. Not everything that is growing in you is for your good. Can you name the things that might be growing in you that can choke God's Word being planted in you?

2. Another way of reading this section is if you are being planted among thorns, are you in the midst of people who are trying to choke what God is sowing in you?

3. What is the Spirit saying to you regarding this text?

Yielding to the Spirit

> Other seed fell among thorns, which grew up
> with it and choked the plants (Luke 8:7).

—*Know*—

If we pay attention to the parable, there is a certain type of procession that is happening as the parable is moving to its final stage. The seed has given purposes—to take root in the soil, spring out of the soil, grow to its full potential, and its final goal is to bear fruit. However, we have discussed certain elements that can hinder such a process. In this particular case, the parable speaks about the thorns.

Later in the text, Jesus explains the parable and He mentions that the thorns are the riches and pleasures of this world that take priority over the fruit of the seed which was planted. According to the explanation, though the seed begins to give some signs of bearing fruit, "the fruit does not mature." In other words, while there are some glimpses of maturity, it is a simple appearance; it does not come to fruition.

—*Be*—

It is hard not to read Jesus' explanation and not think about the encounter of the Rich Young Ruler with the Good Master. In their encounter, the Rich Young Ruler approached Jesus with a pressing question: "Teacher, what good thing must I do to get eternal life?" (Matthew 19:16). I do not have space and time to delve deeply into this story, but for the sake of our discussion, this question opened the door for an interesting conversation that was finalized with the following invitation from Jesus: "If you want to be perfect, go, sell your possessions and give to the poor, and you will have treasure in heaven. Then come, follow me" (v. 21). As we all know, the Rich Young Ruler, saddened by what he heard, walked away.

In a certain way, the Rich Young Ruler wanted to be portrayed at a certain maturity level and shown with a desire to walk a journey that would put him en route to eternal life. However, the seed, though it was giving signs of being fruitful, was choked by the thorns that were also growing in the life of the Rich Young Ruler. His possessions grew stronger than the seed that was planted in him.

—Do—

Let us examine ourselves. Going back to one of the questions above: Can you name the things that might be growing in you that can choke God's Word being planted in you? To be truthful, I am not sure if we can completely get rid of the thorns and the weeds, but we can keep them from growing to the point that they become a hindrance to God's Word in us.

Transparency is a loaded word. I call for vulnerability and the possibility of recognizing things that we do not want to recognize. Yet, that might be the first step toward keeping in check those things that can stop us from following Jesus.

Offer a Prayer

I believe the words of the Psalmist can help us to pray along with him: "Search me, God, and know my heart; test me and know my anxious thoughts. See if there is any offensive way in me and lead me in the way everlasting" (Psalm 139:23-24).

Day 5
A Fruitful Soil

Touching Base

Welcome to Day 5! This lesson marks the end of our first week. As I mentioned in the introduction, I wanted to ap-proach this first week as a way to prepare ourselves for the rest of the study. There are seeds being scattered, and my prayer is, as you read these pages and join with your peers discerning and discussing what is being read, your hearts are being prepared to give a productive and fruit-giving life. To do so, the seed must be nurtured in a fruitful soil, and that is the topic for this week.

Searching the Scripture

> While a large crowd was gathering and people were coming to Jesus from town after town, he told this parable: "A farmer went out to sow his seed. As he was scattering the seed, some fell along the path; it was trampled on, and the birds ate it up. Some fell on rocky ground, and when it came up, the plants withered because they had no moisture. Other seed fell among thorns, which grew up with it and choked the plants. Still other seed fell on good soil. It came up and yielded a crop, a hundred times more than was sown." When he said this, he called out, "Who-ever has ears to hear, let them hear" (Luke 8:4-8).

Answer the Following Questions:

As we approach the end of the first week, ponder the following questions. There is no need to answer them quickly.

1. Does my heart contain good soil that will bring into fruition the seed of the Word?

2. Do people know me by the fruits I bear?

3. What is the Spirit saying to you regarding this text?

Yielding to the Spirit

> Still other seed fell on good soil. It came up and yielded a crop, a hundred times more than was sown (Luke 8:8).

—*Know*—

We finally get to the closing phase of the parable. The bountifulness of the farmer is predicated on the possibilities of finding good soil for the seed that is being scattered. He wants to scatter as much seed as possible. The seed is a good seed and ready to grow and be fruitful. For this to happen, the soil needs to be in good condition, i.e., soil that is not trampled, soil that is not dried, and soil that has been weeded out.

I had mentioned previously, that the seed was a fruitful seed. We know this, because later on, Jesus states the following: "The seed is the Word of God" (Luke. 8:11). What this means is that in even the most precarious terrains, like the rocky and thorny grounds, the seed has the potential to grow. However, the parable makes something clear—that in order to enjoy all the fruitfulness of the seed, it should be planted in good ground. Only then can we be able to reap a plentiful harvest.

—*Be*—

There is something peculiar about the words that Jesus uses as He is telling this parable. As we can imagine, His words are purposely chosen. These words are: along, on, among, and into (ESV). Each one of these words is connected to a specific ground where the seed fell. The seed that was eaten by the birds, fell along the path. The seed that withered fell on rocky ground. The seed that was choked fell among the thorns. Finally, the seed that was a hundred times fruitful fell into the good ground. Let us be that good ground into which the seed of God falls and brings a hundredfold.

—Do—

Now, do not be deceived, as I mentioned in Papito's story, it is not only about having good ground, it is also about working the ground in order keep it good. Hence, we are responsible for maintaining the condition for a plentiful harvest. That is why during His explanation of the parable He states, "But the seed on good soil stands for those with a noble and good heart, who hear the word, retain it, and by persevering produce a crop" (Luke 8:15 NIV). As you can see, there is responsibility in those in whom the seed has fallen. The responsibility is to hear, retain, and persevere. And as a result, the seed will bear fruit.

Offer a Prayer

Dear Lord, I pray that my life be good ground where the seed of the Word of God falls into. But also, I pray that I commit to my responsibilities of hearing, retaining, and preserving the Word that has been planted. So help me, God. Amen!

Group Discussion

Key Scripture: Luke 8:4-8

> While a large crowd was gathering and people were coming to Jesus from town after town, he told this parable: "A farmer went out to sow his seed. As he was scattering the seed, some fell along the path; it was trampled on, and the birds ate it up. Some fell on rocky ground, and when it came up, the plants withered because they had no moisture. Other seed fell among thorns, which grew up with it and choked the plants. Still other seed fell on good soil. It came up and yielded a crop, a hundred times more than was sown." When he said this, he called out, "Whoever has ears to hear, let them hear" (Luke 8:4-8).

Opening—This is a time of fellowship and sharing about one another's lives.

Prayer—Ask the Lord to make His presence known and to begin the process of transformation into Christlikeness for each participant.

Testimony—Ask two or three group members to give a testimony of how God is at work in their lives, whether it is through their daily encounters in this study, or some other way.

Discussion Questions:

1. During the reading of Day 1, it was said that "A Pentecostal learning experience is founded in the Word, guided by the Spirit, and lived out in community." Discuss this in small groups and answer the question: What do you think this means for your community?

2. Why would this farmer scatter seed in such a plentiful way? Why is this important?

3. Take time to expand the relationship between the rocky ground and the Samaritan woman. How does this analogy speak to you? Can you think of another analogy?

4. What type of soil are you? Examine yourself and share your level of soil?

5. The parable ends by stating, "Whoever has ears to hear, let them hear." What are you hearing?

Yielding to the Spirit

Group members should pair off with someone with whom they feel comfortable sharing. Take a moment to remind them of the Group Covenant, particularly the statement on confidentiality. Practice memorizing the key scripture of the week with one another. Then discuss any personal takeaways that you would like your partner to pray about with you. Conclude this conversation by quietly praying for one another. Be attentive to the leading of the Holy Spirit in the use of spiritual gifts. If you do feel led to share something in this way, ask the group leader to come and witness what is being said. This is to provide a reliable witness for all involved.

ENDNOTES
Week One

[1]Leon Morris, *Luke: An Introduction and Commentary*, vol. 3 (Downers Grove, IL, InterVarsity Press), p. 170.

WEEK TWO

～

Walk by the Spirit

WEEK TWO
Walk by the Spirit

Day 1
Introduction

Touching Base

Welcome to Week 2. During our first week, we took time to prepare our hearts for the seed that God is scattering. But as we discussed in the previous week, we do not want to be like the path where the seed fell along the rocky ground, or like the thorns where the seed fell among them. On the contrary, we want to be a ground where the seed can bear fruit like the good soil where the seed fell, producing a hundredfold. In other words, we want to be a fruitful people.

Having this parable as a foundation, the remainder of this study is founded on the words of the apostle Paul written to the Church in Galatia, specifically Chapter 5. As I said previously, Paul is inviting his reader on a journey of bearing good fruit. He states the following, "So I say, walk by the Spirit." And in doing so, we will walk contrary to the desires of the flesh and will be "led by the Spirit" (Galatians

5:18). If we opt to keep walking in the Spirit, we will not act according to the flesh (Galatians 5:19), but we will be on a fruit-giving journey. That is the journey to which the apostle is inviting both the Galatians and us. It is a journey that is characterized by the fruit of the Spirit. Though this week's scripture verses concentrate on verses 16 and 17, I urge you to read the whole chapter as you commit to this study, this will help you get a clearer idea of what God is saying to us through this study.

Searching the Scripture

> So I say, walk by the Spirit, and you will not gratify the desires of the flesh. For the flesh desires what is contrary to the Spirit, and the Spirit what is contrary to the flesh (Galatians 5:16-17).

Answer the Following Questions:

As we approach a new week of study, meditate on the following questions.

1. How can we walk by the Spirit?

2. Why is the Spirit and the flesh counter to each other?

3. Is there any such thing as good desires?

Yielding to the Spirit

> So I say, walk by the Spirit, and you will not
> gratify the desires of the flesh (Galatians 5:16).

—*Know*—

Christ has set us free! What a way to begin the chapter. Those who have responded to the redeeming call of salvation in Christ Jesus are set free. We are free from the bondage of the yoke of slavery guided by the flawed desires and passions of our past human condition.

Today, we are on a new path. Paul makes this point clear by contrasting those who walk by the Spirit and those who keep walking in the desires of the flesh. For Paul, according to the argument in this letter, the foundational characteristic of a fruitful people is that they are guided by the Spirit. As a matter of fact, those who walk by the Spirit can embody the fruit of the Spirit.

—*Be*—

Throughout Chapter 5, Paul uses three unique grammatical constructions when he exhorts his reader about the work of the Spirit in the believer's life. First, he says, walk by the Spirit. Then he states, be led by the Spirit. Finally, he states, live by the Spirit. The last two will be discussed during weeks 3 and 4. For now, we will concentrate on the first.

It seems that those who are in Christ have an undeniable responsibility, that is, according to this passage, not to be passive but to be active. Coming to Christ is not only the turning around from a journey toward damnation, but also the movement toward eternal life with the Godhead. Yet, it is important to note, that though the Galatians are exhorted to do so, it is their responsibility to walk the walk. We have to demonstrate volition—the will to walk.

Two important things need to be said about this particular point. We are not left to ourselves. On the one hand, Paul says that we walk *by* the Spirit. If we will to do so, the Spirit will empower us. The grammatical usage of the phrase "by the Spirit" denotes that "something is done" for someone. In short, if we walk, the Spirit will be with us.[1] On the other hand, we do not have to take on this journey alone, this is very clear in Paul's exhortation. The context of this chapter is predicated on living in the faith community of believers. We are saved into a community; hence, we are not alone. The Spirit and the community will stand by us.

—Do—

Examine yourself. Are you walking? Or, are you passively waiting for something to happen in order to move? Remember, something already happened. Let us say it this way, something has been happening—before creation, in creation, in the cross, in resurrection, and in and through Pentecost. Hence, let us walk, and the Spirit will be by us. Therefore, do not stop and keep walking.

Offer a Prayer

Dear God, pardon me if I have stopped my walk. I commit to keep walking the journey that You have placed me into, and I will trust that Your Spirit will be by me. Amen!

Day 2

Love

Touching Base

Welcome to Day 2! Today, we will begin to look at the different ways that the fruit of the Spirit is manifested in the lives of those who walk by the Spirit. This week we will look at the first three. The other six will be presented during weeks 3 and 4. Day 2 discusses the fruit of love.

Searching the Scripture

But the fruit of the Spirit is **love**, joy, peace (Galatians 5:22).

Answer the Following Questions:

After reading Chapter 5 and meditating specifically on today's text, answer the following questions:

1. Why would you think that Paul begins with love?

2.   Where else does Paul use the word love in Chapter 5?

3.   Why is love so important in our Christian walk?

Yielding to the Spirit

> But the fruit of the Spirit is love, joy, peace
> (Galatians 5:22).

—Know—

It seems that love is a central word in Chapter 5. Paul makes reference to the word love four times—one of them being the key verse for today. Each one has a specific connection and relation to the integral character of the Christian life. The first mention is found in verse 6. The apostle says, "The only thing that counts is faith expressing itself through love." In this particular text, Paul makes a clear connection between faith and love. For him, those who have come to know Christ are embodying their faith— which can also be read as working out their faith—through love. In other words, we know that we believe because love is manifested.

—Be—

Interestingly, the second mention of the word love is mentioned in the context of human relations. Paul is leaving no space for misinterpretation. He states in verse 13, "serve one another humbly in love." Love is demonstrated. Can you recall the opening phrase of John 3:16? It says, "For God so loved the world that he gave his one and only Son." God enacted His love for the world by sending His Son Jesus. Love is not only spoken of; but, love is also demonstrated. Following this line of thought, Paul exhorts his readers that the freedom they have been given should also be demonstrated not through egocentric fleshlike indulgences, but by serving one another in love.

—Do—

The third mention of the word love comes in verse 14. The verse states, "For the entire law is fulfilled in keeping this one command: 'Love your neighbor as yourself.'" Here, Paul is paraphrasing the teaching of Christ. In it, he is confronting the Jews and the Gentiles who are part of the church in Galatia. The former kept the law as their way of living, the latter acclaimed they were adopted by grace. However, both had an unhealthy understanding of law and grace, so Paul challenges them by inviting them to demonstrate law and grace by loving each other by the Spirit. As Ayodeji Adewuya explains, the fruit of the Spirit is "best understood in the context of social relations."[2] Let us go and do the same.

Offer a Prayer

Holy Spirit help me love. Allow my love to express my faith; let my love fulfill both the law and grace; and let my love be demonstrated to others. Amen!

Day 3
Joy

Touching Base

Welcome to Day 3! Today's reading is focused on joy. Joy can be defined as an internal emotion that could be manifested through pleasure and happiness. According to the apostle Paul, this is something that we should experience if we are walking by the Spirit.

Searching the Scripture

> But the fruit of the Spirit is love, **joy**, peace (Galatians 5:22).

Answer the Following Questions:

After reading Chapter 5 and meditating specifically on today's topic, answer the following questions:

1. Are you living joyfully?

2. Is the promise of having joy synonymous to not having difficulties?

3. Share an incident where you experienced joy.

Yielding to the Spirit

> But the fruit of the Spirit is love, **joy**, peace
> (Galatians 5:22).

—Know—

As I thought about this lesson, I could not stop thinking about Paul himself. He was a man who lived a difficult life. His vocation as an apostle to the Gentiles, put him in many difficult situations. Paul was beaten, persecuted, cast away, and imprisoned; nevertheless, as he tells those in Philippi, "whether I am in chains or defending and confirming the gospel, all of you share in God's grace with me (Philippians 1:7). Though in this particular passage, Paul uses the word grace, which is *charis* in Greek, elsewhere, Paul uses a similar phrase to talk about the joy that sustains him, notwithstanding his trials. Interestingly, both grace (*charis*) and joy (*chara*) come from the same root, that is, *chairo*, which means to be glad.

—Be—

When I say that Paul was joyful in the midst of his trials, I do not want to say that we should ignore the difficulties that we are confronting. No! That is to be irresponsible.

What I mean is the contrary. We have to recognize it! We have to stand firm and confront whatever difficulties come toward us. But, if we are walking by the Spirit, the Spirit will bear the fruit of joy in us. It is only then, that we are able to understand what Jesus told His disciples, "But take heart! I have overcome the world" (John 16:33).

—Do—

We can live a joyful life in spite of our trials. I see this very clearly in the life of a very close friend. This friend has en-dured so many difficult events. Even the morning when I was writing this section, I had to pray over the family due to a bad report they had received from the doctor. Yet, as my friend was sharing the news, it was shared with a sense of joy, faith, and trust.

Let us rest upon the Lord. In light of Galatians 5, joy is not dependent on life experiences, but on the Spirit's agency in us. If we walk by the Spirit, we will not only be joyful, but also, we will share the joy.

Offer a Prayer

In this prayer, let the words of the apostle Paul to the church in Corinth serve as a guide: "For our light and momentary troubles are achieving for us an eternal glory that far outweighs them all" (2 Corinthians 4:17).

Day 4
Peace

Touching Base

Welcome to Day 4! "Take a big breath and release it smoothly." Those were the words that my basketball coach would say when I was at the free-throw line. For him, that was his way of helping his players find peace. As I grew older, I learned that is was more than just breathing in and out, it took maturity and God's intervention to be calm in the midst of trials.

Searching the Scripture

> But the fruit of the Spirit is love, joy, **peace** (Galatians 5:22).

Answer the Following Questions:

As you reflect on what it means to walk in the Spirit's peace, answer the following questions:

1. How do you define peace?

2. Share an experience when you were embraced by God's peace?

3. Do you understand peace is something we can attain here and now? Explain how.

Yielding to the Spirit

> But the fruit of the Spirit is love, joy, **peace** (Galatians 5:22).

—Know—

Reflect on the following: How can you enjoy peace if you do not know what it is like to experience difficulties? Or, to muddle the waters a little more, how can we experience peace in the midst of trials? It might be possible that as you are reflecting on these questions or recalling your conversation regarding the questions that were discussed in the previous section, you were not able to define peace or talk about a peaceful experience without mentioning a situation where you felt no peace at all.

Does this mean that peace is only available as a result of tension, difficulties, and problems? No, I do not think so. That would make the fruit of the Spirit contingent to any of those situations. Obviously, we know what peace is as we contrast it with issues like war, tensions, and problems. But believe me when I say, that God's peace can stand, be perceived, and experienced on its own with no further help.

Nevertheless, as it was mentioned in the previous chapter, living in this world will bring its afflictions, yet Jesus has promised peace to us. Not like the peace this world could offer, but the peace that comes from Him.

—Be—

To make things clear, Paul's usage of the word peace (*eirene*) in this passage is not concerning the individual's peace with God or with himself, as important as these are. Paul is actually exhorting the Galatians to have peace with each other. In other words, he is calling them to "harmonious relations and freedom from disputes."

Coming together as community is a very messy task. Just think about those around you. Each person, regardless of being part of a similar class, ethnicity, and context, is raised in a particular way. As a result, life experiences develop in you a certain way of interpreting life. When this is multiplied by ten, thirty or fifty, things can get tense very quickly. Just think about the last time you were around a group of people who tried to come to a consensus about where to eat or where the small group should meet next week. Simple things like these test us. It is in this context that Paul is writing to his readers.

—Do—

Living in peace or doing peace is not an easy thing. Maybe, that is why it is an aspect of the fruit that comes to fruition within those who walk by the Spirit. Though it is a divine grace of the fruit of the Spirit, that does not mean that it is not attainable. The question we need to ask ourselves is: Are we willing to embody God's peace in our interpersonal relationships.

Offer a Prayer

God, help me to not only live in peace with You, but also, let me embody the Spirit's peace in all my relationships.

Day 5
Conclusion

Touching Base

Welcome to Day 5! During this week, we individually studied the first three aspects of the fruit of the Spirit. In this closing chapter, we will briefly review some important things about the fruit, and we will see how these interrelate one to the other.

Searching the Scripture

But the fruit of the Spirit is love, joy, peace (Galatians 5:22).

Answer the Following Questions:

Take time to review what you have discussed in the past couple of days; as you do so, answer the following questions:

1. In what ways has your church community shared their love for you? How have you shared your love for them?

2. In what ways has your church community embodied a joyful attitude for you? In what ways have you shown a joyful attitude for them?

3. In what ways has your church community shown you what it is to live in peace? In what ways have you shown peace to your community?

Yielding to the Spirit

> But the fruit of the Spirit is love, joy, peace
> (Galatians 5:22).

—Know—

It cannot surprise us that Paul anchors this representative list to *agape* (love). On other occasions, when he has listed the word love with other Christian "virtues," Paul has elevated love over the rest. For example, in 1 Corinthians 13, he speaks about the importance of faith, hope, and love in Christlike relationships. However, though all are important, in his final words, he says that love is the greatest of all.

For Paul, as he has said elsewhere, the Christian life happens in God. In his message to those in Athens, as recalled by Luke in Acts 17:28, he lets them know that all creatures live and move in God. For the nonbeliever, that may mean that regardless of their relationship with God, their lives are still within the presence of God. For those who believe, in whom God's love has been poured upon, it means that our lives should be known by that which has been poured into us. Hence, our lives should reflect who God is, and according to 1 John 4:8, that is love.

—Be—

Elsewhere, the apostle Paul says we can rejoice because we have been reconciled through Jesus Christ (Romans 5:11). God's love poured into each believer brings a joyful experience that was not only unknown to us before the Spirit made a home in our hearts through Christ, but now, that which was unknown to us should be an identifying fruit of the Spirit's presence in us.

The joy that Paul speaks about here is predicated in the Spirit. That is why Paul calls the Galatian church to rejoice regardless of the life situations that might hurt, frustrate, or hinder them. As real and concrete as they could be, we are habilitated by the Spirit to rejoice even in our sufferings.

—Do—

The love of God that is in us not only bears the fruit of a joyful heart, but also it should embody peace. Remember, Paul is speaking about communal relationships. Hence, it is important to be in peace with God as with one another. Furthermore, there are two more things that we should have in mind. First, for Paul, peace is holistic in nature; in other words, it is what the Israelites understood as shalom— wholeness. Second, peace is one of the key markers of our kingship with God. This is what Matthew records when he pens the Sermon on the Mount, that those who are peacemakers are blessed because they will be called sons and daughter of God (Matthew 5:9).

Offer a Prayer in Your Own Words

We pray that Your love poured into our hearts may manifest Your joy in us and help us make peace with one another.

Group Discussion

Key Scripture—Galatians 5:22

> "But the fruit of the Spirit is love, joy, peace."

Opening—This is a time of fellowship and sharing about one another's lives.

Prayer—Ask the Lord to make His presence known and to begin the process of transformation into Christlikeness for each participant.

Testimony—Ask two or three group members to give a testimony of how God is at work in their lives, whether it is through their daily encounters in this study, or some other way.

Discussion Questions:

1. How has your understanding of love, joy, and peace been shaped as you finish this week's study?

2. Reflecting on your reading, group discussions, and personal reflections, how much fruit is your life bearing?

3. Is there something that I have left out as an author that has been called to your attention regarding Galatians 5 and the fruit of the Spirit discussed this week?

4. Take time to recall your reading and reflection on this lesson. What is the Spirit showing you?

Yielding to the Spirit

Group members should pair off with someone with whom they feel comfortable sharing. Take a moment to remind them of the Group Covenant, particularly the statement on confidentiality. Practice memorizing the key scripture of the week with one another. Then discuss any personal takeaways that you would like your partner to pray about with you. Conclude this conversation by quietly praying for one another. Be attentive to the leading of the Holy Spirit in the use of spiritual gifts. If you do feel led to share something in this way, ask the group leader to come and witness what is being said. This is to provide a reliable witness for all involved.

ENDNOTES for Week 2

[1]Michael S. Heiser and Vincent M. Setterholm, *Glossary of Morpho-Syntactic Database Terminology* (Bellingham, WA: Lexham Press, 2013).

[2]Ayodeji, Adewuya, *Holiness in the Letters of Paul*, p. 94.

WEEK THREE

❧

Led by the Spirit

WEEK THREE
Led by the Spirit

Day 1
Introduction

Touching Base

Welcome to Week 3. During our first week, we took time to talk about the different types of soils and the importance of preparing our hearts for the seed God is scattering. Last week we explored the first three aspects of the fruit that is mentioned by Paul in Galatians 5:22. These aspects were love, joy and peace. We affirmed that Christ followers should reflect on who God is—love. Also, it was stated that regardless of the difficulties we confront, we are habilitated by the Spirit to rejoice. Finally, it was said that to be in Christ brings peace with God and with one another.

This week we will move to the second triad of aspects of the fruit of the Spirit mentioned by Paul in verse 22—patience, kindness, and goodness. However, before we study these, let us set the context by looking at the second grammatical construction that Paul uses in relation to "walk by the Spirit." In verse 18, instead of using the verb *by* he uses *led*. It seems that the Spirit not only is the source of the walk that Paul is describing, but also the Spirit is the sustenance.

Searching the Scripture

> But if you are led by the Spirit, you are not under the law (Galatians 5:18).

Answer the Following Questions:

As we approach a new week of study, meditate on the following questions.

1. How do you see the Spirit leading you?

2. Are the law and the Spirit contrary to each other?

3. Do you understand the importance of Paul differentiating between walking *by* the Spirit and being *led* by the Spirit?

Yielding to the Spirit

> But if you are led by the Spirit, you are not
> under the law (Galatians 5:18)

—*Know*—

Where the Spirit of the Lord is there is freedom! Can you wrap yourself around this profound proclamation? This is what we can cry out as sons and daughters of God. We are freed from the bondage of the law into the grace of the Spirit. Yet, it seems that some within the Galatian church were falling back into the bondage of the law.

"You were running a good race," says the apostle in verse 8, Who cut in on you to keep you from obeying the truth? By yielding back to the life in the flesh, you become "alienated from Christ; you have fallen away from grace" (Galatians 5:4). They had begun the race with a healthy pace, but they had taken their eyes away from the goal. Paul's words affirm the importance of not only starting right, but also keeping the pace throughout the journey.

—*Be*—

Let us be *led.* The following story will illustrate this point. Recently, the daughter of some friends of ours was running her first cross-country race for the undergraduate institution where she was attending. She had received a full-tuition scholarship from this institution. After the race, she shared that she missed her parents' presence in recent months while preparing for her first competition. She quickly explained what she meant. Her parents always appeared at different points along the race to encourage her. They would say things like, "keep moving," "stretch your arms longer," and "don't lose your step." She missed their support at the beginning of the race, certain points throughout the race to cheer for her, and finally at the finish line to rejoice with her.

We can all agree that it is the daughter who must go through tight spaces, mud, and unlevel terrain. Nevertheless, for her, the voice of her parents at different points in the race helped her keep her stride and not fall back while running toward the goal. To which voices are you paying attention? If you are walking by the Spirit, then you should be led by the Spirit.

—Do—

The same voice that has called us to live in His presence, will sustain us. To be led, is to willingly surrender to the guidance of another. This is what Jesus said about the Spirit when He promised the coming of the Spirit: "But when he, the Spirit of truth, comes, he will guide you into all the truth" (John 16:13).

Offer a Prayer

Holy Spirit, tune my ears to always hear only Your voice. Lead me, Amen!

Day 2
Patience

Touching Base

Welcome to Day 2! We will begin to look at the second triad of aspects of the fruit mentioned by Paul in verse 22. Today, we will look at patience, which can also be defined as patience or long-suffering. I do not know where the Spirit of the Lord wants to take you today, but I pray that this chapter may speak to you as it did to me.

Searching the Scripture

But the fruit of the Spirit is . . . [**patience**], kindness, goodness (Galatians 5:22).

Answer the Following Questions:

After reading Chapter 5 and meditating specifically on today's text, answer the following questions:

1. Do you know someone who exhibits the gift of patience? In what ways have they embodied it?

2. Can you recall a time in His life where Jesus modeled patience?

3. Why is patience important in our Christian walk?

Yielding to the Spirit

But the fruit of the Spirit is . . . [**patience**], kindness, goodness (Galatians 5:22).

—Know—

With the term patience, Paul begins to move into a more ethical practice. In a sense, the first three aspects of the fruit of the Spirit—love, joy and peace—can be understood as gifts that are deposited in us by the Spirit before these are manifested outwardly. If this is true, we can now say that because by the Spirit we are able to love, have joy, and be in peace, we can live in a Christlike manner with one another.

Interestingly, Paul begins with a word that seeks maturity from you and me. We have to embody patience, in other words, the capacity of tolerating and enduring the other. But how shall we tolerate and endure? Such a patience is grounded in the first three words mentioned by Paul—love, joy, and peace.

—Be—

In Isaiah 53:3, the prophet says the following about Jesus, "He was despised and rejected by mankind," and then he also adds, "a man of suffering, and familiar with pain." Hundreds of years before Jesus dwelt with us, it was said that He would suffer, and that pain would be part of His life. But in doing so, according to Romans 8:5, God was demonstrating the love He had for us. "While we were still sinners," Paul continues, "Christ died for us."

These verses serve as examples of patience, though the word is not used in the verse. God's love to humanity was demonstrated through His long-suffering for us. This is the kind of community living that Paul is exhorting, that even though, there may be reasons to do otherwise, taking the long-suffering road of loving the other is what people led by the Spirit do. As I said in the previous section, patience is something that one does for another. However, if all believers have the same attitude of patience, then everyone in the church will be serving each other and becoming "mature, attaining to the whole measure of the fullness of Christ" (Ephesians 4:13).

—Do—

Bearing the fruit of patience testifies that we are led by the Spirit and that we are a fruitful people. As daughters and sons of God, we have received God's mercy (Psalm 103:8); hence, we should give what we have received. By doing so we will be blessed. This is what Jesus told his listeners on the Mount, "Blessed are the merciful, for they will be shown mercy" (Matthew 5:7).

Offer a Prayer

God, I thank You for the gift of patience. Because you embodied long-suffering for us, we received the gift of reconciliation. Help us to be a gift of reconciliation to our community as Your Spirit leads. Amen!

Day 3
Kindness

Touching Base

Welcome to Day 3! Today, we will move to the fifth aspect of the fruit of the Spirit mentioned by Paul in Galatians 5:22—kindness. In a certain way, today's study moves us into action. In other words, kindness is not something that can be done from afar or with arms crossed; it calls for action. We have to move into kindness.

Searching the Scripture

> But the fruit of the Spirit is . . . [patience], kindness, goodness (Galatians 5:22).

Answer the Following Questions:

After reading Chapter 5 and meditating specifically on today's text, answer the following questions:

1. When you hear the word kindness, can you picture someone in your life that models it?

2. Share an experience where you were the recipient of someone's kindness.

3. If you agree that kindness is an action, give an example.

Yielding to the Spirit

> But the fruit of the Spirit is . . . [patience], kindness, goodness (Galatians 5:22).

—Know—

Kindness is something that we decide to show to others regardless of their actions. Just as God showed us patience, He also has embodied kindness to all human beings. In Psalm 34:8, the writer says the following, "Taste and see that the Lord is good; blessed is the one who takes refuge in him." Though the version that I am using for this book uses the word "good" in Psalms 34:8, in the Septuagint, the Greek word used to translate "good" is *chrestos*, which is a variation of the word Paul uses in Galatians 5:22, *chrestotes*. Hence, the psalmist invites us to taste and see that God is kind. Kindness is an attribute of God.

Moreover, the kindness of God is not contingent on who we are. That is, there is not much we can or cannot do to affect God's kindness. Regardless of what we do or not do, God is kind. That is who God is, and what God is, is what He does. This is what Luke says when he narrates the words of Jesus himself in Luke 6:35-36:

> But love your enemies, do good to them, and lend to them without expecting to get anything back. Then your reward will be great, and you will be children of the Most High, because he is kind to the ungrateful and wicked. Be merciful, just as your Father is merciful.

—*Be*—

As I think about this word, Mia Kamila comes to mind. Mia Kamila is the middle child God gave our family. When she was in second grade, she went through a battery of exams in order to find out why she was having difficulties in reaching the education goals for a child of her age. After many exams, Laura and I were told that her diagnosis was a speech impediment—her challenge was how to process the information she was receiving. As she grew older and became more aware, she became more frustrated about it.

Mia Kamila has never hated school. On the contrary, she enjoys going and letting other gifts flourish as she battles with her speech impediment. For her, that gift is kindness. One of the constant ways that her teachers and school staff describe her is as a "kind" person. According to them, she goes out of her way to serve those who might be struggling more than she is. She has her own struggles, but this does not stop her from showing kindness. Furthermore, these children do not have a way of paying her back; but regardless, Mia Kamila does what she does, because that is who she is.

—Do—

Mia Kamila's story challenges me, I can sit and excuse myself from sharing whatever gifts I have until my problems are resolved. Yet, in her case, embodying kindness is not dependent on resolving her issues. It flows out of who she is. We should do the same.

Offer a Prayer

Let us repeat the words of Jesus and let them be our prayer for this day: "Blessed are the merciful, for they will be shown mercy." Amen!

Day 4
Goodness

Touching Base

Welcome to Day 4! Today will end the second triad of aspects of the fruit of the Spirit presented by Paul. We began this second triad with a study of the term patience. Then, we looked at kindness. Today, we move toward goodness. According to those who have studied this text, we should understand goodness as generosity. Those who are led by the Spirit are generous with one another. And those who are generous, are givers—according to the apostle Paul: "God loves a cheerful giver" (2 Corinthians 9:7).

Searching the Scripture

> But the fruit of the Spirit is . . . [patience], kindness, **goodness** (Galatians 5:22).

Answer the Following Questions:

After reading Chapter 5 and meditating specifically on today's text, answer the following questions:

1. In what way has God been generous to you?

2. How does your church community embody the gift of generosity?

3. Recall a moment when you were generous to someone. What was their reaction? How did you feel?

Yielding to the Spirit

> But the fruit of the Spirit is . . . [patience], kindness, **goodness** (Galatians 5:22).

—*Know*—

Agathosyne, the Greek form that Paul uses for goodness is found only four times in the New Testament. All four occur within the Pauline writings (Romans 15:14, Galatians 5:22, Ephesians 5:9; and 2 Thessalonians 1:11). Though all follow the same context found in the Galatian passage—

that of being generous—it is interesting that in the Ephesian passage Paul also correlates goodness with a characteristic of the fruit of the Spirit. He states the following:

> For you were once darkness, but now you are light in the Lord. Live as children of light (for the fruit of the light consists in all goodness, righteousness and truth) and find out what pleases the Lord. Have nothing to do with the fruitless deeds of darkness, but rather expose them (Ephesians 5:8-11).

Furthermore, in this passage, as it happens in Galatians 5, Paul contrasts between those who are in darkness and those who are in the light. He begins Chapter 5 by exhorting those at Ephesus to follow God's example and walk in love. Those who do so, are children of the light. For Paul, living in the light will naturally bear fruit and will help us find what pleases the Lord. In order to make his point clear, Paul describes that kind of living consists of embodying goodness, which is generosity.

—Be—

The first image that might come to our minds when we think about goodness and generosity is that of a wealthy person giving to those who are in need. Without questioning that image, generosity also goes beyond the financial capabilities of an individual or community. Generosity takes many forms and shapes.

In the last couple of days, I have been remembering the life of a man named Carlos Seda. As I was writing this week's study, I was notified that Carlos passed away. We met when I was in my early teens. I do not remember how

Carlos and his family arrived at our church, but they did so in a time of need.

We were about to begin a construction project, and out of nowhere God brings Carlos—a veteran of the Vietnam War. As soon as he knew about the construction project, he approached the pastor and said that he was willing to lead the project as he had experience as a construction foreman, and he was willing to do it pro bono. Carlos did not have much history in our church. He did not have a story about how our church helped him in a certain moment and this was his way of paying it back. He offered himself. Literally, one day he walked to the front of the church took the offering plate, which was placed on the altar, and stepped into it and said, "I do not have money, but I offer myself."

What Carlos did for our church was out of generosity. He did it because he was a generous man. Although I do not know how he found out about our church, I can say that he was led by the Spirit. He offered his time, hands, and knowledge to a community that had not done anything for him—that is goodness.

—Do—

What do you have? That is the question that Jesus asked the disciples when the multitude was hungry. It might take some searching and discernment. Take time to do it. Are you willing to step into the plate? God will bless whatever we have and use it for the benefit of those around you.

Offer a Prayer

Holy Spirit, ignite in me a spirit of kindness. Take what I am and use it for the service of others. Amen

Day 5
Conclusion

Touching Base

Welcome to Day 5! During this week, we individually studied the second triad of characteristics listed by Paul. In this closing chapter, we will briefly review some important things about each of them and also, we will see how these connect.

Searching the Scripture

> But the fruit of the Spirit is . . . [patience], kindness, goodness (Galatians 5:22).

Answer the Following Questions:

Take time to review what you have discussed in the past couple of days, as you do so, answer the following questions

1. List the ways in which your church or community has modeled patience to you. In what ways have you modeled patience to the church or community?

2. List the ways in which your church or community has embodied kindness. In what ways have you embodied kindness?

3. List the ways in which your church or community has shown what it is to be generous. In what ways have you shown generosity?

Yielding to the Spirit

> But the fruit of the Spirit is . . . [patience],
> kindness, goodness (Galatians 5:22).

—*Know*—

Living in community is hard. We are constantly tested by other styles and forms of thought. This was one of the main issues that Paul was facing when he wrote to the Galatians. That is the reason why Paul asked them, "Who cut in on you?" There was tension between the Jews and the Gentiles. Should circumcision be practiced or not? Would it be better to be under the law or grace? Understanding this reality, Paul not only called them to follow what he already had taught them, but also to practice patience, i.e., to patiently live with one another.

—*Be*—

One way of living patiently with one another is by practicing kindness. As we discussed earlier in the week, kindness is something we decide to show to others regardless of their actions. One thing I did not mention then, that I would like to raise in this conclusion is that the Greek word for kindness is built upon the term *chrestos*, which was used for naming a common slave. In other words, to be kind is to serve others. Moreover, there is a similarity with the word *Christos*, which is the Greek word for Christ. Christ is the suffering servant; He is the one who willingly came to serve the Father and creation in the power of the Holy Spirit. Hence, it is not surprising that Christians were called to be *Chrestos* as *Christos* is.

—*Do*—

One way of showing kindness is by being generous. It is interesting that when I was writing about the topic of goodness, I remembered the self-giving attitude of Carlos. Similarly, in Isaiah 63, the prophet calls God's people to remember what the Lord did for them. One of the things that Isaiah exhorts them to remember is the Lord's goodness: "Yes, the many good things he has done for Israel (Isaiah 63:7).

Be led by the Spirit, and as you go, let patience, kindness, and goodness speak of the fruit of the Spirit that is in you.

Offer a Prayer in Your Own Words

Lead me, and I will follow. Lead me into patience, lead me into kindness, and lead me into goodness. This I ask! Amen.

Group Discussion

Key Scripture—Galatians 5:22

> "But the fruit of the Spirit is . . . [patience], kindness, goodness."

Opening—This is a time of fellowship and sharing about one another's lives.

Prayer—Ask the Lord to make His presence known and to begin the process of transformation into Christlikeness for each participant.

Testimony—Have two or three group members give a testimony of how God is at work in their lives, whether it is through their daily encounters in this study, or some other way.

Discussion Questions:

1. How has your understanding of patience, kindness, and goodness been shaped as you finish this week's study?

2. Reflecting on your reading, group discussions, and personal reflections, which of these do you believe you need to practice more?

3. Take time to recall your reading and reflections on this lesson, what is the Spirit showing you?

4. How do you see the first set of three words connecting to the second set of words that we studied this week?

Yielding to the Spirit

Group members should pair off with someone with whom they feel comfortable sharing. Take a moment to remind them of the Group Covenant, particularly the statement on confidentiality. Practice memorizing the key scripture of the week with one another. Then discuss any personal takeaways that you would like your partner to pray about with you. Conclude this conversation by quietly praying for one another. Be attentive to the leading of the Holy Spirit in the use of spiritual gifts. If you do feel led to share something in this way, ask the group leader to come and witness what is being said. This is to provide a reliable witness for all involved.

WEEK FOUR

❧❦

Live by the Spirit

WEEK FOUR

Live by the Spirit

Day 1

Introduction

Touching Base

Welcome to Week 4. This will be our final week together. As a way of connecting the dots, let me share a short summary of what we have done to this point. During week 1, we studied the importance of preparing our hearts in order to receive the seed that is being scattered and bear a hundredfold. In Week 2, we studied the first three aspects of the fruit of the Spirit found in Galatians 5:22—love, joy, and peace. In a way, these serve as a foundation. Last week, Week 3, we studied the second aspects of the fruit of the Spirit—patience, kindness, and goodness. It was said that those who are full of the Spirit's love, joy, and peace will be led by the Spirit to embody practices such as kindness, patience, and goodness.

This week we will discuss the third and final triad mentioned by Paul. These are found in verses 22 and 23—faithfulness, gentleness, and self-control. Prior to doing so, let us set the context by looking at the third grammatical construction that Paul uses in relation to the phrases— "walk by the Spirit" and "led by the Spirit." In verse 25, Paul uses the following phrase—"live by the Spirit." For Paul, those in whom the Spirit has been planted live a certain way; that is, according to the Spirit.

Searching the Scripture

> Since we live by the Spirit, let us keep in step with the Spirit (Galatians 5:25).

Answer the Following Questions:

As we approach a new week of study, meditate on the following questions.

1. In your own words, explain the uniqueness of using "walk, led, and live."

2. How do you keep in step with the Spirit?

3. Paul does not leave you alone, he writes in plural form—"we live" and "let us keep." How important is this for you?

Yielding to the Spirit

> Since we live by the Spirit, let us keep in step with the Spirit (Galatians 5:25).

—*Know*—

Have you ever been in a familiar setting and all of a sudden, you see someone that you rarely see but it seems like someone you know? As you inquire about who that person is, you find out that he or she is closely related to someone you know. Let us say that she is the daughter of a church friend who is back from college and you had never met her. Nevertheless, because she is blood related, she may look like your friend; because, she was raised in the same household, she acts similarly to your friend; and many other things that could be named. Why does this happen? The amount of time they spent together shaped them. They are family.

I ended the section named "touching base" affirming that people who are indwelt by the Holy Spirit must live according to the One who indwells them. For Paul, there could be no distance between what happens internally in us and what happens externally. There must be congruency between the source, the sustenance, and the course. Hence, the difficult question that we need to ask ourselves is: Are we spending time with the Spirit?

—Be—

It is hard to speak about this and not think about Peter. After Jesus was arrested, Peter followed from a distance until he walked into the courtyard of the high priest's house (Luke 22:54). Peter was not there by himself, other people were in the courtyard sitting near a fire that was kindled. All of a sudden, a servant girl passed by, and she saw something in Peter that connected him to Jesus. As a result, she stated, "This man was with Him" (Luke. 22:56). As we know, Peter denied his relationship to Jesus. He denied Jesus three times. The first two was due to something they saw in Peter. The third one, mentioned he spoke like a Galilean. That means that he heard something that reminded him of Jesus.

Peter was not raised by Jesus, but he spent the last three years of his life walking, eating, resting, ministering, talking, and doing life with Jesus. That interrelated experience between Peter and Jesus was so profound that Peter did not need to say much for people to recognize him as one who walked with Jesus. Even when he spoke, it also connected him.

—Do—

It seems that for Paul there is a close connection between the indicative and the imperative. If you Galatians indicate that you live in the Spirit, says Paul, then it is imperative that you follow the step of the Spirit. Now, the flip side of what Paul is saying is, if your walk is not up to step with that of the Spirit, you cannot say that you are living in the Spirit. Consequently, if the Spirit is not guiding your steps, then the flesh becomes your guide.

Offer a Prayer

Lord, let our actions, words, and lives become a sign of Your presence in us. We do not want to lose step with the Spirit, but on the contrary, we want to live by it. Amen!

Day 2
Faithfulness

Touching Base

Welcome to Day 2! Today, we begin with our final triad of words. This triad begins with the term faithfulness. It is important to remember the context of the text. On one hand, Christians are empowered by the Spirit to embody each aspect of the fruit of the Spirit. On the other hand, these are lived out within the community. This last point is very important in order to understand Paul's use of faithfulness. Paul is not expecting that Christians place in one another the same faith that they placed in God. But he does expect that those who live by the Spirit are people of trustworthiness.

Searching the Scripture

> But the fruit of the Spirit is . . . **faithfulness**,
> gentleness and self-control (Galatians 5:22-23).

Answer the Following Questions:

After reading Chapter 5 and meditating specifically on today's text, answer the following questions:

1. Why is it important to not confuse faith in God with faithfulness with one another?

2. What are the characteristics of a trustworthy person?

3. Does trustworthiness mean that the community will always do what you want?

Yielding to the Spirit

> But the fruit of the Spirit is . . . **faithfulness**,
> gentleness and self-control (Galatians 5:22-23).

—Know—

This final section on the fruit of the Spirit takes us to a more inward turn. It invites the hearers to self-evaluate themselves in areas of great importance. Though Paul is speaking to a community of listeners, he is also approaching each individual with each word that he was using. In this specific case, the question is: Are you trustworthy? It is not if others will be trustworthy with you; but rather, if you are a dependable person for others. Can your brother or sister come to you with a situation knowing you can be trusted?

According to Chapter 5, Paul has become worried because some members of the Church in Galatia are listening to voices that are not trustworthy, and by doing so, that which Paul had taught them has become a questionable topic. In response, Paul appeals to them on the basis of the content of the message that he preached to them and also in the trust that he has in them: "I am confident in the Lord that you will take no other view" (Galatians 5:10). For Paul, this is a very important topic. Personally, he has constantly defended his apostleship of Christ. If there is something that he is not willing to compromise, it is his trustworthiness, because it was central to his testimony and to his vocation as an apostle of Christ.

—Be—

If there is a constant theme that summarizes the criticism that I have heard over the years from people who had negative experiences in the church it is that of trust.

I would hear things like, "The church left me hanging" or "I will never trust in that church anymore." What I find interesting about this is that one of the most used slogans by Christians is, "God will never fail you." But when we use these sort of slogans, we forget that the church is part of that equation. As F. F. Bruce states, "Because God is faithful, because he can be relied upon, his people are to be faithful too, and the Spirit enables them to be so."[1]

—*Do*—

Please, do not stop preaching and proclaiming that God is faithful. His faithfulness is not contingent on ours. God's faithfulness is God's Godness. But be mindful of this, that when we proclaim God's faithfulness, we are responsible to do our part, even if it seems insignificant. If so, we might be blessed enough to hear God say, "Well done, good and faithful servant! You have been faithful with a few things; I will put you in charge of many things. Come and share your master's happiness!'" (Matthew 5:23).

Offer a Prayer

In a world where people have grown weary of trusting each other, I pray that in the power of the Holy Spirit, that I become a trustworthy gift to those who come to me. Amen!

Day 3
Gentleness

Touching Base

Welcome to Day 3! After discussing the giftedness of being a trustworthy person, today we will study the word gentleness. By gentleness, the text means the ability to be gentle, meek, or a person who is even-tempered

Searching the Scripture

But the fruit of the Spirit is . . . faithfulness, **gentleness** and self-control (Galatians 5:22-23).

Answer the Following Questions:

After reading Chapter 5 and meditating specifically on today's text, answer the following questions:

1. Does being gentle mean that we are easy to manipulate? Explain.

2. Did you know that the gentle Christians are promised the inheritance of the Earth? Find the scripture and give the reference.

3. Can you name someone who embodies this fruit?

Yielding to the Spirit

> But the fruit of the Spirit is . . . faithfulness, **gentleness** and self-control (Galatians 5:22-23).

—*Know*—

The Greek term that Paul used for gentleness is *prautes*. This term has three main definitions: humility, humble, and gentle. Though Paul has written elsewhere about the importance of being humble and having humility

(Philippians 2), in this particular passage, the biblical scholars agree that the use of gentle or meekness might be preferable.

It seems that the Church in Galatia was lacking a gentle character and they were attending to some issues harshly. For example, if we go to Chapter 6, Paul tells them the following when he recommends how to care for someone who has been caught in sin, "You who live by the Spirit should restore that person gently" (Galatians 6:1). As you can see, Paul reinforces in Chapter 6 what he is exhorting them to do in Chapter 5. Gentleness cannot be hindered by the acts of the other, gentleness is a fruit of those who live by the Spirit.

—Be—

To be gentle is not to be someone who is constantly a target of manipulation. Very clearly Jesus told His disciples something like, be inoffensive as doves, but astute as snakes. In other words, the presence of a meek character does not presuppose the absence of being prudent. However, the former goes far beyond the latter. That is why, when Jesus shared the values of the kingdom of God at the beginning of His public ministry on Earth, among many other things, He said the following about those who embody a gentle spirit, "Blessed are the meek, for they will inherit the earth" (Matthew 5:5).

—Do—

The enacting of gentleness takes humility. But, this is what we are called to do. If we are Christians and we see ourselves as living Christlike lives, then there is no escape.

Elsewhere in Matthew, Jesus expresses the following: "Learn from me, for I am gentle and humble in heart" (Matthew 11:29). To take the cross is to do what Christ did. But by doing so, rather than embodying weakness, we embody meekness and a kind of power that is contrary to what this world seeks.

Offer a Prayer

In Psalms 37, the psalmist states that the meek shall inherit the land. With this in mind, let us use verses 27 and 28 as our prayer for today. Turn us from doing what is bad and help us to do good; by doing so, we will dwell in the land forever. For the Lord loves the just and will not forsake His faithful ones..

Day 4
Self-Control

Touching Base

Welcome to Day 4! We have reached the final aspect of the fruit of the Spirit mentioned by Paul to the church in Galatia. Its placement to the end of the list does not mean that it is less important than the rest. Actually, though we read them in a sequential order, this does not mean that these are manifested in some sort of progression. Hence, the importance does not rely in the order they are manifested, but in knowing they are part of our Christian walk.

Searching the Scripture

But the fruit of the Spirit is . . . faithfulness, gentleness and **self-control** (Galatians 5:22-23).

Answer the Following Questions:

After reading Chapter 5 and meditating specifically on today's text, answer the following questions:

1. Is self-control something that impacts the individual or the community as a whole? Explain.

2. Are you prepared to walk according to God's will?

3. What it the Spirit telling/ministering to you?

Yielding to the Spirit

> But the fruit of the Spirit is . . . faithfulness, gentleness and **self-control** (Galatians 5:22-23).

—*Know*—

The Word itself is clear in denoting that this aspect of the fruit is experienced inwardly. It is the sole resolution of not giving in to whatever negative desires may be present in your life. It is not a surprise to read such a word in the Pauline letters. Being a student of Greek philosophy, Paul had known the powerful virtue of being able to resist any sort of temptation. For some of these teachers, self-control was the cusp of all virtues.

Though self-control is an act that in principle seems only beneficial to the individual; however, we must not overlook that it also has community implications. If not, Paul would not have mentioned it in the context of this exhortation. When an individual gives in to his or her desires (I am not only speaking about sexual desires, but also fleshly desires contrary to the Spirit) it would not take long before we would see how such an act will impact the community of this individual. As a matter of fact, if we continue reading from Chapter 5 to 6, what follows is Paul's exhortation for acting gently when someone from within the community has acted selfishly and has been caught committing sin. Although it is one who could not practice self-control, the whole community is affected and called upon in the process of restoration.

—Be—

Let us flip the coin and see self-control through a positive lens. This will be an important exercise because self-control does not only impact us when someone indulges their desires, but it also impacts the community when we choose to exercise control.

Recall Jesus' prayer at the Garden of Gethsemane where Jesus is close to His arrest, imprisonment, trial, and death. His prayer reveals the agony that He will suffer in the journey that is ahead of Him. Hence, in the midst of the prayer, Jesus cries out the following words, "Father, if you are willing, take this cup from me; yet not my will, but yours be done" (Luke 22:42). Sometimes, it is hard for us to imagine Jesus' humanity. Jesus was not immune to being tempted. Actually, the Book of Hebrews says that Jesus was tempted in every way; however, He did not yield to such temptations (see 4:5). In a way, His public ministry began when the Holy Spirit led Jesus to the desert, and there He was tempted by the devil. But He did not give in. Fast-forward three years, and now we find Jesus about to fulfil His mission as the slain Lamb of God and in His prayer, He asks the Father to pass this cup from Him. But immediately, Jesus recalls that His will is not to be done, but that of the Father.

—Do—

Those who live by the Spirit, do not seek their will but the will of the Father. To practice self-control is to abstain from indulging into fallen desires and to rest in the goodness of God's will. I know that it is not easy. Even Paul recognizes it: "For I do not do the good I want to do, but the evil I do not want to do—this I keep on doing" (Romans 7:19); but immediately, just as Jesus did, Paul states, "Thanks be to God, who delivers me through Jesus Christ our Lord!" (Romans 7:25).

Offer a Prayer

I recognize that this is a very important but personal matter. Take time to think about the area or areas where you need to practice self-control, and if possible, write your own prayer below:

Day 5
Conclusion

Touching Base

Welcome to Day 5! This week we studied the final three aspects of the fruit of the Spirit listed by Paul in Galatians 5:22-23. This concluding chapter will highlight some important characteristics within this triad and see how they interconnect with each other.

Searching the Scripture

> But the fruit of the Spirit is . . . faithfulness, gentleness and self-control (Galatians 5:22-23).

Answer the Following Questions:

Take time to review what you have discussed in the past couple of days. As you do so, answer the following questions:

1. How well does the church embody a trustworthy presence?

2. In what ways is the church helping in modeling a gentle Spirit in a hostile environment?

3. How do you see your church doing God's will?

Yielding to the Spirit

But the fruit of the Spirit is . . . faithfulness, gentleness and self-control (Galatians 5:22-23l.

—Know—

We all are seeking relationships with people and communities that are trustworthy. The entertainment world realized this and quickly took advantage. In the late 1990s and early 2000s, the concept of reality TV recaptured the prime time hours of the major TV networks. Still today, there are some airing. Although I do not follow many of the reality shows that air on regular or cable networks, I am a fan of movies and shows based on real events. There is something interesting about watching a story, which even though is being portrayed by actors and actresses, is based on a story that happened in a certain place and to certain people at some time in history.

The challenge with both the reality shows and the productions based on real events is that due to the nature of the industry, there are events that might be tweaked to manipulate the story for the sake of creating a major impact. Once the viewer becomes aware of that, discouragement might set in.

Something similar happens between the church community and those who see us from afar. Just as we are able to find out what is true and what is not in TV shows and movies, people are able to find out when Christians are not trustworthy. As God's people, we need to examine ourselves and seriously ask the following question: Are we portraying our Christian communities as trustworthy? Another equally vital question is: Are we portraying our Christianity as trustworthy to our communities?

—Be—

I do not know if you can agree, but I find that we are living in a time where hostility has become the new normal. As a result, gentleness seems like a trait in extinction. It seems like hostility is met with hostility and meekness is a sign of weakness. But the body of Christ has been called to model something different. The writer of the Proverbs states the following, "A gentle answer turns away wrath, but a harsh word stirs up anger" (Proverbs 15:1).

As Christians, we are not only responsible for being a community that embodies trust, but also, we should be a community that instead of igniting the fire of hostility should be agents of humility. As Paul himself said, "Do not let any unwholesome talk come out of your mouths, but only what is helpful for building others up according to their needs, that it may benefit those who listen" (Ephesians 4:29).

—Do—

Finally, the church is also responsible for practicing self-control. It is very easy to forget this and believe that the church has been called into existence to be self-serving. But the church must do as Jesus did in the Garden of Gethsemane—she cannot focus on her own will, but live in the will of the One who called her into existence.

As a Spirit-filled community, we ought to live out each of the Spirit's fruit. By doing so, the world will know that God has sent us. And as Paul concluded, "Against such things there is no law" (Galatians 5:23).

Offer a Prayer

Dear God, as we come to a close, I pray that my heart has become good soil for the seed You are planting in us. And I pray that as I walk by the Spirit I am led by the Spirit; and live by the Spirit; and my life will bear a hundredfold greater outflowing of love, joy, peace, patience, kindness, goodness, faithfulness, gentleness, and self-control. Amen!

Group Discussion

Key Scripture—Galatians 5:22-23

"But the fruit of the Spirit is . . . faithfulness, gentleness and self-control."

Opening—This is a time of fellowship and sharing about one another's lives.

Prayer—Ask the Lord to make His presence known and to begin the process of transformation into Christ-likeness for each participant.

Testimony—Have two or three group members give a testimony of how God is at work in their lives, whether it is through their daily encounters in this study, or some other way.

Discussion Questions:

1. As we come to a close, what have you learned throughout this journey?

2. Take time to reflect on your life and each of the aspects of the fruit of the Spirit that we have studied. Which ones are you living out and which ones do you have to practice more?

3. How has your understanding changed of what it is like to live in the Spirit?

Yielding to the Spirit

Group members should pair off with someone with whom they feel comfortable sharing. Take a moment to remind them of the Group Covenant, particularly the statement on confidentiality. Practice memorizing the key scripture of the week with one another. Then discuss any personal takeaways that you would like your partner to pray about with you. Conclude this conversation by quietly praying for one another. Be attentive to the leading of the Holy Spirit in the use of spiritual gifts. If you do feel led to share something in this way, ask the group leader to come and witness what is being said. This is to provide a reliable witness for all involved.

ENDNOTES Week 4

[1] (F. F. Bruce, *The Epistle to the Galatians: A Commentary on the Greek Text*, p. 254).

BIBLIOGRAPHY

Adewuya, Aydoeji. *Holiness in the Letters of Paul*, (Eugene, OR: Wipf and Stock Publishers, 2016).

Allen, John. *National Catholic Reporter* (January 28, 2008) *ncronline.org/news/if-demography-destiny-pentecostal-are-ecumenical-future*, accessed, July 25, 2015.

Bruce, F.F. *The Epistle to the Galatians: A Commentary on the Greek Text* (Grand Rapids, MI: Wm.B. Eerdmans Publishing Co., 1982).

Granberg-Michaelson, Wesley. "Future Faith: Ten Challenges Reshaping Christianity in the 21st Century." Church of God *Evangel* (March 2019, Cleveland, Tennessee: Pathway Press) 9.

Heise, Michael S. and Vincent M. Setterholm. *Glossary of Morpho-Syntactic Database Terminology* (Bellingham, WA: Lexham Press, 2013).

Lugo, Luis. Spirit and Power: A 10-Country Survey of Pentecostals, *pewforum.org/files/2006/pentecostals-08.pdf.* accessed July 20, 2015.

Martin, Ralph. *The Catholic Church at the End of the Age: What the Spirit Is Saying*, (San Francisco: Ignatius, 1994).

Morris, Leon. *Luke: An Introduction and Commentary*, Vol. 3, (Downers Grove, IL: InterVarsity Press, 2008).